T0196247

THE UNUSUAL CHILDHOOD OF

Daisy the
Baby Hawk

The Unusual Childhood of
Daisy the
Baby Hawk

Anne R. Hughes

THE UNUSUAL CHILDHOOD OF DAISY THE BABY HAWK

iUniverse books may be ordered through booksellers or by contacting:

iUniverse
1663 Liberty Drive
Bloomington, IN 47403
www.iuniverse.com
1-800-Authors (1-800-288-4677)

ISBN: 978-1-4917-7170-9 (sc)
ISBN: 978-1-4917-7171-6 (e)

Print information available on the last page.

iUniverse rev. date: 07/06/2015

Contents

Dedication

This book is dedicated to my wonderful son, Matt Hughes. He entered mine and his father's life like a shooting star from Heaven. Like me, he has scaled many mountains and landed on his feet. He is a talented artist, musician, and now businessman. He has illustrated three of my previous books and provided the cover for this book. He has truly blessed my life.

Foreword

Anne is a dear friend who I refer to as "my other mother". This feeling is mutual as she considers me "another daughter". We have one of those friendships that you can't quite remember how it began. It was instant. I learn more about her each time we visit and have determined that two qualities have helped her succeed in life: her faith and her humor.

Her life began in Daytona Beach, Florida, but after several moves, college, many years of teaching, a marriage and a son, Anne now resides in Atlanta at Budd Terrace nursing home. One should know however, that Anne has lived an extraordinary life and has lived it to the fullest. After a shocking accident in her 30's, she was paralyzed from the waist down; but after much hard work and encouragement from The Sheppard's Spinal Clinic, she was able to move on with her life. My "other mother" was not only 1st runner up and Ms. Congeniality in the Ms. Georgia Wheelchair Pageant, but also nominated by Max Cleland to receive the Georgia Handicapped Women of the Year Award. I am proud to say that she in fact received that award.

I'm sure Anne has experienced many tough days and situations but one would never know this about her. She gives positive words to all she meets. She's a popular resident of Budd Terrace where she loves and is loved by many of the staff and residents.

The poems to follow are a wonderful representation of Anne's humorous side. She reads them with a smile, a chuckle in her voice, and a sparkle in her eye. Despite her situation, she is still able to be young at heart.

--Laura

A Note from Anne

This endeavor is an effort of much love and hours of hard work. A special thanks for the funding of this book goes to George Flanagan and the Joy Boys, Susan Snyder, Donna Myrick, Suzy Jennings, Anne Allan, Virginia Knox, Minnie Foster, and Beverly Willingham.

Others who have been there with much encouragement through all of my books are my son, Matt, my sisters Jean Eickhoff, Sue Tetterton and their families, Gail Goldberg, Betty Williams, Alicia Starr, Beth Mahaffey, Glen and Jean Robertson, Robert Koehler, and Dr. and Mrs. Carroll Hughes.

A special note for my wonderful editor, Laura Roberts, who also wrote the forward and who has recently completed her master's degree in music therapy.

For spiritual support I thank Rev. Diana and Jim Roberts and my dear lion Max Cleland.

Anne R Hughes
2014

The Ballad of
Daisy-The Baby Hawk

I have a baby hawk. Her name is Daisy.
She sits on a limb, and is kind of lazy.

She's a jolly little bird, but all she says is, "Peep!"
Her favorite pastime is to ride in my jeep.

She often hunts squirrels, holds the meat in her cheek,
And uses their tails to clean her beak.

I love little Daisy. She's not at all mean.
And I just call her my squirrely machine.

The Anaconda

There was an anaconda who lived in a deep, dark lake.
And was very handsome, for a great, long snake.

He played football on the lake's rocky beach,
And liked to scare swimmers who would run and screech.

He wore a cool jacket and a red cap too,
And he gave his class ring to his girl, Betty Lou.

So if you find an anaconda, don't you put him in a zoo.
'Cause if you are not careful, you could be there too!

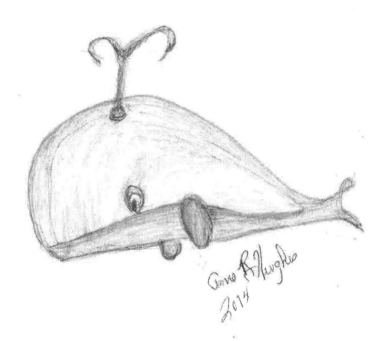

The Whale

There was a whale who was a detective,
Who lived in the ocean pit.
Who always said while solving a case,
"I know that you know who did it."

He found that there was gold missing
From the pirate's kit,
And he always said to the suspect,
"I know that you know who did it."

He was called to solve a murder.
A frog had murdered a tic.
And the detective always said,
"I know that you know who did it."

He received a reward for his efforts
For the way he made everything fit.
After receiving the key to the ocean he said,
"I know that you know who did it."

Allowishes

Allowishes is a camel I know.
He doesn't do dishes and moves rather slow.

He's a funny ole cad and has two big humps,
But cries out in pain when he hits many bumps.

He played a key note in a Christmas play,
But chewed up a wise man when he tried to pray.

So get you a camel if you run out of gas.
You'll go ten miles per hour, but this too shall pass.

The Bat

I knew a bat
His name was Dave.
Said he was only looking
For a cave.

I knew of one
On Crabgrass Hill.
Dark and deep
And very still.

Dave worked at night
For a medicine man.
He gathered blood
In a big tin can.

So if you love bats
Go to a deep, dark cave.
Check around
And ask for Dave.

The Piranha

There was a piranha who was all alone
Who said to all he saw, "I'll take the skin off your bone."

He lived in an underground cavern, a place he called home.
And he said, "Come over here. I'll take the skin off your bone."

He called the shark up on the phone
And said, "Come over my way-I'll take the skin off your bone."

So if you like piranha, but like all of you home.
You hear them whisper,
"Come over here. I'll take the meat off your bone."

Anne K O'Loughlin
2014

The Cow

There is a special cow.
Anna Masie is her name.
She sings beautiful songs
That are never the same.

She's in love with a bull.
His name is Horny Sam.
Anna says, "Whenever he comes,
You know where I am."

Anna and Horny have a small business.
They make Blue Bell cheese.
They know you'll be happy,
And it makes them pleased.

So go find a cow
Who gives all she's worth.
And before you know it,
She'll even give birth.

The Goat

There is a goat whose name is Mary Lou,
Who said, "Go, go, go to your waterloo!"

She chewed on boxes and old, old shoes
And said, "I'll go, go, go to my waterloo!"

This little goat worked in a hospital and sometimes a zoo
And always said, "Go, go, go your waterloo!"

So if you like little goats and big goats too
You will hear them say, "Go, go, go to your waterloo!"

The Duck

I have an ole duck, his name is Jack,
But all he likes to do it quack.

He has really flat fee and loves to dance-
Doesn't like to leave much to chance.

So get you a duck, but don't make duck stew.
He could be me, he could be you!

Anne B. Hughes
2014

The Polar Bear

You have heard that Polar Bears are becoming extinct.
I'm here to tell you that you can alleviate this problem.
All you have to do is get you a great big ole Polar Bear
And put him in your bed on a cold winter's night
And bury your nose in his thick warm fur.
And on a hot summer's night
It is often refreshing
To feel his warm, fish scented breath
Blowing softly on your face.
So get you a big old Polar Bear
And see what you've been missing!

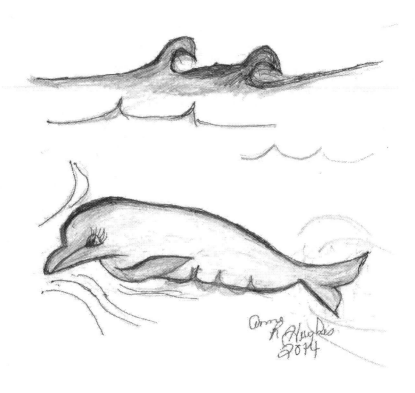

The Dolphin

There was a little dolphin who swam for a mile.
Who could plant a kiss on you and make you smile.

She would find stranded sailors who were lost at sea
And would give them hope and would make them feel free.

She brought strength to the weary, a star for the weak,
New wishes for the little ones, lovely words for the old to speak.

So go find a dolphin under the sea,
She'll bring a smile to you and a promise to me.

The Inch Worm

There was an inch worm
Who moved very slow,
But she was very reliable
As inch worms go.

She was hired by the University
To teach calculus and measures,
And found she spent many hours
Studying the museum's many treasures.

She measured sculptures and landscapes too.
She measured many portraits and a petting zoo.

Her most famous measurement
Was of an antique desk
Which had hidden compartments
Where ancient treasures did rest.

In one of the desk compartments
Was an ancient scroll.
It told of a locked room
Where good and evil took their toll.

The little inch worm decided
There are some things best not to measure.
When you know this,
Only then can you find your treasure.

Anne R. Hughes
2014

The Jellyfish

There was a little jellyfish who was only a pup,
Who always said, "Give it up. Give it up!"

He lived in a lab in a deep cup,
And he said to all who came by, "Give it up. Give it up!"

The scientists ran experiments on this little pup,
And all he would say is, "Give it up. Give it up!"

The little jellyfish wanted to go to the ocean.
He was tired of the dark cup.
And all he would say is,
"Ya'll, give it up!!"

The Kitten

I know a kitten named Mr. Pywacket.
He's not at all quiet and makes lots of racket.

He takes each corner at a 60 miles per hour tear.
He loves to play fetch and toss balls in the air.

He's a regular sweetheart and I love that kitty so.
He was my baby before I had one and that feeling did grow.

One night he got sick with a bad kidney stone,
And we were in the hospital and felt all alone.

My wonderful husband came up that night,
He said that everything would be alright.

The vet said Pywacket's little body was sore.
He just couldn't stand to hold on anymore.

We buried our kitty who had many charms
In a small box down on the farm.

So if you meet a fun kitty who always likes to play,
Then this really could be your very finest day.

The Moth

There was a moth, her name was Cindy.
She lived in a valley that was very windy.

She painted portraits of the valley creatures.
Some clients were doctors, others were teachers.

Her most famous art was the valley queen.
A buxom beauty named Jeneen.

So if you love good art, go to a valley that's windy,
Check around and look for Cindy.

Anne R Hughes
2014

The Cricket Charmer

There once was a cricket charmer whose name was Shining Bright.
And she tantalized all with her singing all day and all night.

She had a love interest whose name was Darkness Fell.
They had a baby charmer who joined their chorus well.

The three called themselves Charmed By Night.
And to all who would listen, they made everything right.

The Kangaroo

I know a kangaroo
Whose name was Mae.
She kept busy teaching kindergarten
And this job filled her day.

The little school was located
Across many hills,
And she gleefully hopped over them
Without many spills.

One day she came to a rainbow
Whose vivid colors took her breath away,
Jumping made her feet so happy
She decided to stay.

The Mouse

There was a twister chaser, a mouse named Long Tall Sallie
Who studied tornadoes through every crook and alley.

She was an expert on twisters as all she knew could see.
She watched barns burning and saw them uproot every tree.

She saw homes demolished, cows fly through the night.
'Cause twisters wreaked havoc and always started a fight.

Sallie was known as an authority, recognized wherever she roamed.
This mouse was always a drifter with no place she called home.

So if you like Sallie when twisters come near
You can be sure there will always be one less thing to fear.

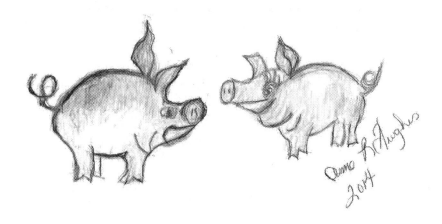

The Pig

I know a pig whose name is Peanut.
When she goes out she likes to play Putt-Putt.

She uses a curling iron to curl her tail,
And likes to eat corn in a big tin pail.

She loves to live down on the farm,
And has made herself a beautiful room in the barn.

So if you need a friend, it could be a pig
Who makes you so happy you dance a little jig.

The Chipmunk

There was a chipmunk with very fat cheeks
Who carried his food heavy and deep.

He played his guitar for a country music band,
And his songs were famous all through the land.

He sang of his hero-Merl the Toad
Who helped the weary down the small town road.

So if you like chipmunks find a country music band
And one will tell you of his hero and take your hand.

Tony

I have a friend.
A pony named Tony.
He gets really mad
When you call him a phony.

He feeds on oats,
But I make oatmeal cookies instead.
He says something sweet
Really goes to his head.

When your bottom gets sore
And you can't bend over,
You may wish you could land
In a bed of clover.

So get you a pony
That's not too slow
Who really takes off
When you say... "GO!"

The Crab

There once was a crab named Rufus
Who rode seahorses in the ocean's races.

He set quite a record and became a legend
Which was talked about in many places.

Rufus had a girlfriend whose name was Louie Lu.
She cooked Rufus' favorite meal which was made of seaweed stew.

So if you love crabs who can make you smile,
You can often find them in less than a mile.

The Scorpion

There was a certain scorpion
That climbed many mountains high.
Some of the tallest seemed
To even reach the sky.

He found a falcon's nest
And an eagle's nest too.
In one he found eggs
And a buttoned up shoe.

He ran into squirrels,
Chipmunks, and geese.
He found that climbing
Really brought him peace.

So if you like mountains
And scorpions too
You'll find that the next climber
May even be you.

The Birth of the Starfish

There was a little twinkling star that looked for a home in the sky,
And waved at the bigger stars as they passed by.

They thought her magnificent because she was so small.
They laughed at her and mimicked her and never, ever would call.

The Papa of the Heavens looked down from up above
And decided to send this sad child down to the ocean for love.

He threw this little star....
And gave her a special kiss and that's how the starfish was born.

The Stingray

There was a stingray who lived in the deep
And made all he met sob and weep.

He had a lethal stinger he used on all he met
Which made him a creature you'd never forget.

He sent many to the hospital, many to the shore,
Many to the graveyard 'till they weren't anymore.

He was hateful and wild, a creature so mean
And was known to all as the killer machine.

Anna R Hughes
2014

The Tapeworm

I've got a tapeworm. His name's Shalome.
Said he was only looking for a home.

How could I have bargained for this
Growing bigger by the minute is really the pits!

Baby-you gotta get outta here!!

The Crocodile

Rambo Doodle is a crocodile who walks like a man.
He can cover ten miles just about any way he can.

He rides a white pony and motorcycle too.
He'll outsmart me and hoodwink you.

The legend of Rambo Doodle spreads far and wide.
He covers every inch of the country side.

So go find Rambo Doodle. Look near and far.
You may even find him riding in a car.

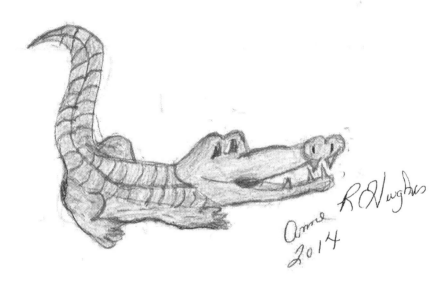

Anne R Vaughns
2014

The Tiger

I ride a tiger who thinks he's a cat.
So what can you possibly think of that?

His name is Vincent and he loves to hunt.
People really hurt him when they call him a runt.

He's five foot six and light on his feet.
Who would think a tiger could be so sweet?

So get you a tiger who loves you like crazy
Who can learn to fetch and never get lazy!

Printed in the United States
By Bookmasters